T0195704

# SPANISH-ENGLISH
# HANDBOOK
## FOR MINISTRY AND MISSIONS

*Reaching People for Christ in Spanish and English*

## KIMBERLY WHITE

WESTBOW
P R E S S®
A DIVISION OF THOMAS NELSON
& ZONDERVAN

WestBow Press books may be ordered through booksellers or by contacting:

WestBow Press
A Division of Thomas Nelson & Zondervan
1663 Liberty Drive
Bloomington, IN 47403
www.westbowpress.com
844-714-3454

Because of the dynamic nature of the Internet, any web addresses or links contained in this book may have changed since publication and may no longer be valid. The views expressed in this work are solely those of the author and do not necessarily reflect the views of the publisher, and the publisher hereby disclaims any responsibility for them.

Any people depicted in stock imagery provided by Getty Images are models, and such images are being used for illustrative purposes only. Certain stock imagery © Getty Images.

Scripture quotations marked NIV are taken from The Holy Bible, New International Version®, NIV® Copyright © 1973, 1978, 1984, 2011 by Biblica, Inc.® Used by permission. All rights reserved worldwide.

El texto Bíblico marcado NVI ha sido tomado de la Santa Biblia, NUEVA VERSIÓN INTERNACIONAL® NVI® © 1999, 2015 por Biblica, Inc.® Usado con permiso de Biblica, Inc.® Reservados todos los derechos en todo el mundo.

Scripture marked (KJV) is taken from the King James Version of the Bible.

Scripture quotations marked (RVR 1960) are from the Reina Valera © 1960. El texto Biblico ha sido tomado de la version Reina-Valera © 1960 Sociedades Biblicas en America Latina ; © renovado 1988 Sociedades Biblicas Unidas. Utilizado con permiso.

ISBN: 978-1-9736-8861-7 (sc)
ISBN: 978-1-9736-8863-1 (hc)
ISBN: 978-1-9736-8862-4 (e)

Library of Congress Control Number: 2020904865

Print information available on the last page.

WestBow Press rev. date: 11/19/2021

# CONTENTS

# INTRODUCTION

In November 2007, I took an opportunity offered by my church to go on my first mission trip to Mexico. I had been a church member for about four years. Year after year, I had heard about and seen my sisters in Christ going on mission trips. I had been a master's degree student in Mexico almost eight years prior but assumed I would only use the Spanish I learned then to teach students English and communicate with their parents; this was my field of expertise. But the call to missions had started when I was a little girl filling boxes with my mother which we gave to people poorer than us in and around our community. And there was a tug at my heart: God wanted me to go back to Mexico to help with the group from my church who were going on their second or third trip. I was frightened, but I went. As soon as I arrived, I learned I was only one of three or four U.S. Americans on the trip who knew enough Spanish to translate or attempt to translate. Again, I was scared.

But God had prepared me through a few prior experiences: working with immigrant families who aspired to become U.S. citizens, working with employees at the university I got my Master's degree from, taking Spanish for two years in college, and learning Spanish on my own. Even with fear in my heart, I knew I had to obey the tug on my heart. So, I went on my first trip. On that trip, I was assigned as an encourager and a translator. I was excited to help my group by talking to people in the street and translating for our team and our Mexican companion churches' team. I knew a few words for prayer, a few words to use to ask people to please come to the church, but fewer words for ministry terms though, since my strongest technical Spanish vocabulary was for use in my career in education. But the weekend trip was going pretty well, and I felt good after a couple of days. I felt like that trip was the first time in my life where so many skills I had acquired through almost 14 years of post-secondary education were used. I translated, taught, talked to people, sang as part of worship, and just felt joy that I was helpful and useful.

When Sunday came, I saw one of my fellow translation assistants be assigned to do translation work at another church, and I was puzzled. The pastor had told us the day before he would need someone to translate for him, and this sister had been with him for many years before me. She had led worship, and she had a reasonable control of Spanish. Wasn't the pastor who led the group going to need a translator as he had told us the night before? Oh, I reasoned, there is our fluent Mexican-American brother who knows both Spanish and English; he must be the one who will translate. But then I was called down to the pastor's office to speak with him, and my stomach began to turn. What would he be calling me for a couple of hours before he preached?

I went into the office and sat down in a blue chair. He asked if I had a Spanish bible. Yes, I had one. He then asked if I would translate at church that morning. No isn't an answer when you are asked by a man of God on the mission field to do something, no matter how poor you think your skills are to do it. I had enough excuses to fill a bucket, but I knew he didn't have many other people to pick from, from so yes was the answer.

I remember standing on a wooden stage beside the man of God; I wore a pink shirt and long brown skirt. I had never preached, nor had I ever been asked to translate for anyone who was preaching anywhere. But I had watched my mother. I watched her give speeches with enthusiasm, inflection, and love for God's word. She didn't worry, or if she did, I never knew it. She did it as naturally as if it were breathing. I can't say my first time doing it I was like her. My heart beat fast, but I did it. I didn't have words for a lot of terms I had never needed to use, but I got help.

"Be encouraged," the pastor shouted. So, encouraged, I prayed that the audience would have more English than I had Spanish. I could hear someone shout something from the audience, but it wasn't clear. "Be encouraged," the pastor implored again. I thought: "God, please help me; I don't know what that word is. I have never used it before." Then I heard more clearly: "Sea animado." "Oh, that's what that means," I thought, and then repeated what I heard. I leaned not into my own understanding, but listened for help throughout that sermon, as will you. Even if you look or feel foolish, look to the audience to help you if they can. Find a paraphrase if you can. Use this book when you can. I hope and pray you will find your experiences using Spanish in a Christian context to be a lot easier with the help of this book. May God bless you and help you as you begin, continue, or expand your knowledge of Spanish.

# Why a Linguistic Guide for Christian Ministers and Missionaries?

The purpose of this book is to help English speakers integrate Spanish into their communications with people to demonstrate God's love to Spanish speakers. It is also intended to help Spanish speakers know the words to express themselves and show God's love to English-speaking Christians better. With lists of useful vocabulary, it is hoped this book can be used to reach believers and nonbelievers from Spanish-speaking countries. I hope that through this guide, beginning missionaries, English-speaking pastors, and congregations who want to minister to Spanish-speaking populations can attain an understanding of the Spanish language and use it in ministry work. I also hope that the reader will gain an understanding of the language and cultures of many different Spanish-speaking groups to promote ministries that build upon the cultural assets of the Spanish-speaking populations they want to minister to.

Language learning involves learning to listen and understand a language, learning to speak a language, and learning to read and write a language. If you plan to minister to Spanish-speaking populations that have little or no formal education, your primary goals will be to learn to listen, speak, and understand a language. If you plan to participate in Spanish-speaking services, as well as minister to and assist Spanish-speaking churches and clergy, you should also learn vocabulary that will help you to read the Bible, hymns, and written materials. This will allow you to participate in worship with them as well as help them reach others with some education.

For centuries, English-speaking Christians have gone into Spanish-speaking countries to bring the Word of God to populations with histories of practicing the occult, devil-worshiping, ancestor worshiping, and other forms of worship that keep them disconnected from God, His love, and His salvation. Most of these Christians went into the cultures with good intentions, but they brought not only the Word of God; they also brought their own language, culture, and beliefs. They wanted to show Christ to the people who did not know him but often did not consider the language, cultures, and ways of thinking of the people they intended to help. Due to their lack of cross-cultural understanding, they sadly experienced miscommunication and cultural clashes that negated the beauty of these cultures, which were not necessarily ungodly.

Rather than seeing cultural and religious beliefs as two things that needed careful marrying, these missionaries introduced the love of God into the communities while also sometimes imposing their own cultural belief systems. They did this without understanding how to consider the elements of who these people were and the parts of their culture that did not interfere with the worship of God. Now with much new information on how to help understand and integrate cultural understanding in the world, including in educational venues and religious ones, we can now integrate language and culture to help new believers understand how the love of God doesn't negate their cultural background but embraces it. It does not require the abandonment of one's native language but allows for integrating new terms and concepts into one's language to express God's love and embrace of all the languages he created and the peoples he loves so much. Jesus commanded his followers:

> Therefore, go and make disciples of all nations, baptizing them in the name of the Father and of the Son and of the Holy Spirit, and teaching them to obey everything I have commanded you. And surely, I am with you always, to the very end of the age. (Matthew 28:19–20 NIV)

Or in Spanish:

> Por tanto, vayan y hagan discípulos de todas las
> *naciones, bautizándolos en el nombre del Padre
> y del Hijo y del Espíritu Santo, enseñándoles a
> obedecer todo lo que les he mandado a ustedes. Y
> les aseguro que estaré con ustedes siempre, hasta el
> fin del mundo. (Mateo 28:19–20 NVI)

**Language Learning: Do I have the time?**

Language learning takes time and dedication. When we learn
our first languages, also known as native language or home language,
we learn them from the people in our family, in our immediate
home, and in our surroundings. As the cliché goes, children appear
to absorb language like sponges just by being present in a place
where people speak the language. It is also common that multiple
languages will be spoken in the same home. Children can easily
acquire two, three, or even four languages if they hear and use the
languages daily.

You will find that some Spanish speakers speak multiple
languages, some indigenous to their local ethnic group and others
imported through past colonization of the country. Some people
will use Spanish as a language of religion and speak other languages
at home, in the market, and even another language in government
offices. Because of this, Spanish speakers will have varying proficiency
in each language they speak. When passing out tracts and literature,
it is possible that the people may not be able to read any of it. That
is why it is important that you speak to them as well.

You will experience different levels of success than others who
are attempting to learn the same language depending on certain
factors. If you have teens trying to learn Spanish for ministry, they

may learn it at a much quicker rate than young adults and older people will. Also, they may sound a lot better and communicate better with native speakers of the language. Generally, language-learning research shows that older learners who have never learned a language before may experience difficulties pronouncing unfamiliar sounds in the new language. You may have difficulty hearing the difference between, for instance, the *n* in *nada* and the second *n* in *niño*. You might also have difficulty pronouncing the *r* in *rojo* and the *r* in *arête*.

While you study, you should pray that God will make known to you your linguistic strengths and allow you to use them for his glory. You should pray that God will allow you to hear and use the new sounds and vocabulary from the language you are learning. Also, pray that God will speak through you and use your tongue and vocal cords to help you speak and be understood. There may be times when you speak Spanish and don't know exactly what you are saying or where it came from, but that comes with praying that God will use you as his vessel and allowing him to do so. Just beginning the journey to learn Spanish shows God your dedication to him and your dedication to the people he loves.

Studying any language will take time and discipline. Do not get in a hurry to learn unless you are willing to put in the hours of study needed to learn quickly. Language learning takes time and patience. If you put in the time, pray about it, and be patient; God will help you understand the materials in this language-learning guide.

# EXPLANATION OF ABBREVIATIONS

I have chosen to include a few abbreviations in this book. For example, the use of *m* or f after a word stands for masculine or feminine. In Spanish, nouns generally have a masculine and feminine form. For the masculine noun, use a masculine article in front. For the feminine noun, use a feminine article in front.

**Masculine forms**

El libro is the book.

Un libro is a book.

**Feminine forms**

La gata is the cat.

Una gata is a cat.

Adjectives can have masculine and feminine forms as well. If the form changes for adjectives behind feminine nouns, the feminine form is included in parenthesis after the masculine form. Many times it is just an added *a,* instead of the *o* that is generally used in masculine forms.

(n) (v) (adj) (adv)

The parts of speech are included after some words. Nouns generally have one form, and verbs have many forms depending on tense and aspect. Consult a good grammar book to refine your ability to speak and write with different verb tenses. Generally, the infinitive or the form of the verb that has *to* in front of it (e.g., to go; to carry) in English is used in this guide. You can use a Spanish dictionary and add this information for yourself where I haven't if you find that helpful.

# Books of the Bible: The Old Testament

| | |
|---|---|
| Genesis | *Génesis* |
| Exodus | *Éxodo* |
| Leviticus | *Levítico* |
| Numbers | *Números* |
| Deuteronomy | *Deuteronomio* |
| Joshua | *Josué* |
| Judges | *Jueces* |
| Ruth | *Rut* |
| I Samuel | *I Samuel* |
| II Samuel | *II Samuel* |
| I Kings | *I Reyes* |
| II Kings | *II Reyes* |
| I Chronicles | *I Crónicas* |
| II Chronicles | *II Crónicas* |
| Ezra | *Esdras* |
| Nehemiah | *Nehemías* |
| Esther | *Ester* |
| Job | *Job* |
| Psalm | *Salmo* |
| Proverbs | *Proverbios* |
| Ecclesiastes | *Eclesiastés* |
| Song of Solomon | *Cantar de los Cantares* |
| Isaiah | *Isaías* |
| Jeremiah | *Jeremías* |
| Lamentations | *Lamentaciones* |
| Ezekiel | *Ezequiel* |
| Daniel | *Daniel* |
| Hosea | *Oseas* |

| | |
|---|---|
| Joel | *Joel* |
| Amos | *Amós* |
| Obadiah | *Abadías* |
| Jonah | *Jonás* |
| Micah | *Miqueas* |
| Nahum | *Nahum* |
| Habakkuk | *Habacuc* |
| Zephaniah | *Sofonías* |
| Haggai | *Ageo* |
| Zechariah | *Zacarías* |
| Malachi | *Malaquías* |

# Books of the Bible:
# The New Testament

| | |
|---|---|
| Matthew | *Mateo* |
| Mark | *Marcos* |
| Luke | *Lucas* |
| John | *Juan* |
| Acts | *Hechos* |
| Romans | *Romanos* |
| I Corinthians | *I Corintios* |
| II Corinthians | *II Corintios* |
| Galatians | *Gálatas* |
| Ephesians | *Efesios* |
| Philippians | *Filipenses* |
| Colossians | *Colosenses* |
| I Thessalonians | *I Tesalonicenses* |
| II Thessalonians | *II Tesalonicenses* |
| I Timothy | *I Timoteo* |
| II Timothy | *II Timoteo* |
| Titus | *Tito* |
| Philemon | *Filemón* |
| Hebrews | *Hebreos* |
| James | *Santiago* |
| I Peter | *I Pedro* |
| II Peter | *II Pedro* |
| I John | *I Juan* |
| II John | *II Juan* |
| III John | *III Juan* |
| Jude | *Judas* |
| Revelations | *Apocalipsis* |

# WHO IS GOD TO CHRISTIANS?

| | |
|---|---|
| Advocate | *Defensor* |
| Alpha and Omega | *el Alfa y la Omega* |
| Ancient of Days | *un Venerable Anciano* |
| Banner | *bandera, plancarta* |
| Comforter | *edredón (bed, blanket)* |
| Counselor | *Consolador, Asesor* |
| Defender | *Defensor* |
| Deliverer | *Repartidor, Liberador* |
| Doctor | *Doctor* |
| Encourager | |
| Everlasting Light | *Luz Eterna* |
| Father, Holy Father | *Padre, Padre Santo* |
| Father, Son, and Holy Ghost | *Padre, Hijo, y Espíritu Santo* |
| Friend | *Amigo* |
| God | *Dios* |
| | *Dios Omnipotente, Dios Todopoderoso* |
| God Almighty | *Dios que me ve* |
| God Who Sees Me | *Digno* |
| Good | *Grandioso, mas que bueno* |
| Great | *Sanador, Curandero* |
| Healer | *lugar de escondite* |
| Hiding Place | *Altamente exaltado* |
| Highly exalted | *Padre Santo* |
| Holy Father | *Santo de los santos, El Sanctasanctórum* |
| Holy of Holies | *Dios Santo de Israel* |

| | |
|---|---|
| Holy One of Israel | *La Santísima Trinidad* |
| Holy Trinity | *Esperanza* |
| Hope | *Esposo* |
| Husband | *Rey* |
| King | *Rey de Reyes* |
| King of Kings | *Abogado* |
| Lawyer | *Agua Viviente* |
| Living Water | *El Señor de Todo* |
| Lord of All | *El Señor de Señores* |
| Lord of Lord | *Paz* |
| Peace | *Príncipe de Paz* |
| Prince of Peace | *Proveedor* |
| Provider | *redimir (sinner)* |
| Redeem | *Redentor* |
| Redeemer | *Roca, Peñón* |
| Rock | *Salvador* |
| Savior | *Refugio, Cobijo* |
| Shelter | *Escudo* |
| Shield/Buckler | *Torre fuerte* |
| Strong Tower | *Dios eterno* |
| The Everlasting God | *El Señor* |
| The Lord | *El Señor es nuestra salvación.* |
| The Lord is Our Righteousness | *Aquí habita el Señor* |
| The Lord is There | *La Verdad* |
| The Truth | *Tremendo (m)* |
| Tremendous | *Maravilloso* |
| Wonderful | *el Labrador* |
| The Gardener | |

# WHO WAS JESUS ON EARTH?

| | |
|---|---|
| Jesus | *Jesús* |
| Christ | *Cristo* |
| king | *Rey* |
| son of God | *Hijo de Dios* |
| living word | *Palabra Viviente* |
| The way, truth, and the light | *El Camino, La Verdad, y La Luz* |
| teacher | *Maestro* |
| prophet | *Profeta* |
| Messiah | *Mesías* |
| the lamb[17] | *el cordero* |
| shepherd[18] | *el pastor* |
| the son of man[19] | *el hijo de hombre* |
| The First and the Last[20] | *el Primero y el Ultimo* |
| The living one[21] | *el que vive* |
| The Lion of the tribe of Judah[22] | *El León de la tribu de Judá* |
| The heir to David's throne[23] | *la Raíz de David* |
| Faithful and True[24] | *el testigo fiel y veraz* |
| The Word of God | *La Palabra de Dios* |
| King over all Kings | *Rey de reyes* |
| Lord over all Lords | *Señor de Señores* |
| The Alpha and the Omega | *el Alfa y la Omega* |

[17] Revelations 5:6
[18] Revelations 7:17
[19] John 6:27, Revelations 1:13
[20] Revelations 1:17
[21] Revelations 1:18
[22] Revelations 5:5
[23] Revelations 5:5
[24] Revelations 3:14

| | |
|---|---|
| The beginning and the End | *el Principio y el Fin* |
| The Bright Morning Star | *la brillante estrella de la mañana* |
| Bread of Life[25] | *Pan de la Vida* |
| Light of the World[26] | *Luce del Mundo* |
| Gate for the Sheep[27] | *la puerta de las ovejas* |
| Good Shepherd[28] | *buen pastor* |
| The resurrection and the life[29] | *la resurrección y la vida* |
| Mediator[30] | *mediador, arbitrador,* |
| | *conciliador, intercesor,* |
| | *intermediario, negociador* |
| The true vine[31] | *la vid verdadero* |

[25] John 6:35
[26] John 6:35
[27] John 10:7
[28] John 10:11
[29] John 11:25
[30] 1 Timothy 2:5-6
[31] John 15:1

# WHO/WHAT IS THE HOLY SPIRIT?

| | |
|---|---|
| Holy Spirit | *Espiritu Santo* |
| The Spirit | *El Espíritu* |
| The Spirit of God | *El espíritu de Dios* |
| The breath of the almighty[32] | *El alentó del Todopoderoso* |
| The spirit of fire[33] | *El espíritu de fuego* |
| The spirit of judgment[34] | *El espíritu de juicio* |
| The spirit of truth[35] | *El espíritu de la verdad* |
| The spirit of wisdom | *El espíritu de sabiduría* |
| The spirit of understanding | *El espíritu de entendimiento* |
| The spirit of counsel | *El espíritu de consejo* |
| The spirit of power | *El espíritu de poder* |
| The spirit of knowledge | *El espíritu de conocimiento* |
| The spirit of the fear of the Lord[36] | *El espíritu de temor del Señor* |
| The oil of joy[37] | *El aceite de alegría* |
| The spirit of glory | *El espíritu de la gloria* |
| The spirit of grace | *El espíritu de la gracia* |
| The Eternal Spirit[38] | *el espíritu eternal* |
| The Counselor[39] | *el asesor* |
| seven spirits[40] | *siete espíritus* |

[32] Job 33:4
[33] Isaiah 4:4 from http://www.godonthe.net/HolySpirit/snames.htm
[34] Isaiah 4:4
[35] John 14:17; John 15:26; John 26:13
[36] Isaiah 11:2
[37] Hebrews 1:9
[38] Hebrews 9:14
[39] John 14:26; John 15:26; John 16:7
[40] Revelations 1:??

# WORSHIP AND PRAISE EXPRESSIONS

| | |
|---|---|
| bless | *bendecir* |
| bow | *inclinar* |
| confession | *confesión* |
| creed | *credo* |
| everlasting | *eterno* |
| exalt | *exaltar, engrandecer* |
| excellent | *excelente* |
| exceptional | *excepcional* |
| faithfulness | *fidelidad* |
| fantastic | *fantástico* |
| glorify | *glorificar* |
| great | *bueno* |
| hallelujah | *hallelujah* |
| highly exalted | *altamente exaltada* |
| hymn | *himno* |
| incredible | *increíble* |
| marvelous | *maravilloso* |
| outstanding | *destacado* |
| powerful | *poderoso* |
| Praise God | *Alabar a Dios* |
| Praise the Lord | *Alabar al Señor* |
| precious | *precioso* |
| psalm | *salmo* |
| remarkable | *extraordinario* |
| right | *correcto (ta), bueno (a)* |
| righteous | *justo (a), honrado (da)* |
| righteously | *honradamente, con rectitud* |
| sacrifice | *sacrificar* |

| | |
|---|---|
| service | *servicio* |
| thank you | *gracias* |
| thankful | *agradecido* |
| thankfulness | *agradecimiento* |
| tremendous | *magnífico* |
| worship | *adoración, culto* |

### *How to Praise God*

| | |
|---|---|
| with music | *con música* |
| with our tongues | *con nuestras lenguas* |
| with thanksgiving | *con gracias* |
| through poetry | *a través de poesía* |
| through meditating on his word | *a través de meditar en su palabra* |

# REQUESTS

| | |
|---|---|
| anoint | *ungir* |
| break down *(doors or barriers)* | *echar abajo* |
| breakthrough | *gran avance* |
| consecrate | *consagrar* |
| courage | *coraje (anger or courage)* |
| discipline | *disciplina* |
| eternal life | *vida eterna* |
| forgive | *perdonar a alguien* |
| God fearing | *temeroso(sa) de Dios, piadoso (sa)* |
| godliness | *devoción (f) piedad (f)* |
| godly | *piadoso(sa), Pío(a), Divino(a)* |
| have mercy | *tener compasión de* |
| help me | *ayuda me* |
| listen to me | *escucha me* |
| miracles | *milagros* |
| signs | *signos* |
| strength | *fuerza, fortaleza* |
| strengthen | *fortalecer* |
| wonders | *maravillas* |
| Your will be done | *Hágase tu voluntad* |

# MINISTERIAL NEEDS FOR BELIEVERS AND NON-BELIEVERS

| | |
|---|---|
| assure | *asegurarle* |
| confirm God's wor**d** | *confirmar la palabra de Dios* |
| encourage | *animarle* |
| explain | *explicar* |
| guide | *guiar* |
| help | *ayudarle* |
| identify | *identificar* |
| motivate | *motivarle* |
| reward | *recompensarle* |
| strengthen | *fortalecerle* |
| suggest | *sugerir* |
| support | *apoyarle* |
| thank | *agradecerle* |

# Types of Ministries

| | |
|---|---|
| Agricultural | *agricultura* |
| Business | *Negocios/comercios* |
| Children's Ministry | *Ministerio de niños* |
| Church Planting | *Plantador de iglesias* |
| Computers and Internet | *Computadora e Internet* |
| Counseling | *Consejeria* |
| Discipleship | *Discipulado* |
| Education | *educación* |
| Evangelism | *Evangelismo* |
| Leadership Training | *entrenamiento para lideres* |
| Media and Publication | *Medios y publicacion* |
| Medical Support Staff | *Personal de apoyo médico* |
| Medicine | *Médicina* |
| Prayer Walks | *Caminatas de oración* |
| Short-term coordinator | *Coordinador a corto plazo* |
| Student/Youth Work | *Estudiante/Trabajo juvenil* |
| | *Enseñanza del inglés como* |
| TESL/TEFL | *segunda lengua/ Enseñanza del* |
| | *inglés como lengua extranjera.* |
| Translation/Linguistics | *traducción y lingüística* |
| Women's Ministry | *Ministerio de mujeres* |

# PRAYER

| | |
|---|---|
| prayerful (adj) | *Devoto (adj) Devot(a)* |
| to pray about somebody | *orar por alguien/rogar a alguien* |
| give | *dar* |
| prayer | *oración, rezar (switched spots)* |
| They prayed to God. | *Ellos estaban orando a Dios. Le rezaron a Dios.* |
| She was saying her prayers. | *Ella estaba diciendo sus oraciones.* |
| prayer service | *Estaba rezando sus oraciones.* |
| prayer book | *Servicio de Oracion* |
| Lord's Prayer | *devocionario, libro de oraciónes* |
| Holy Scripture | *oración del Señor* |
| Holy Bible | *sagradas escrituras* |
| | *la Santa Biblia* |

# BIBLICAL AND WORLD TIME AND TIME EXPRESSIONS

### Basic sentences for talking about time

| | |
|---|---|
| We are going to the church at … | *Estamos yendo a la iglesia en…* |
| | *Vamos a ir a la iglesia a las …* |
| We are going to start at … | *Vamos a empezar a las …* |
| What time is it? | *¿Qué hora es?* |

| | |
|---|---|
| afternoon | *tarde* |
| in the afternoon | *En la tarde/ por la tarde* |
| this afternoon | *esta tarde* |
| tomorrow afternoon | *Mañana en la tarde/ mañana por la tarde* |
| dawn | *amanecer* |
| day | *día* |
| all day long | *todo el día* |
| evening | *tarde* |
| | *noche* |
| in the evening | *En la noche/ por la tarde* |
| this evening | *esta tarde* |
| tomorrow evening | *Mañana en la noche/ mañana por la tarde* |
| midnight | *Medianoche* |
| at midnight | *a la medianoche* |
| morning | *Mañana* |
| in the morning | *En la mañana/ por la mañana* |
| this morning | *esta mañana* |
| tomorrow morning | *mañana por la mañana* |

| | |
|---|---|
| night | *Noche* |
| at night | *Por la noche/ de noche* |
| last night | *Anoche* |
| tonight | *esta noche* |
| tomorrow night | *mañana por la noche* |
| noon | *mediodía* |
| at noon | *al mediodía* |
| sunrise | *salida del sol* |
| sunset | *puesta del sol* |
| time | *tiempo* |
| time (hour) | *Tiempo (hora)/ hora* |
| time (once, twice) | *tiempo (una vez, dos veces...)* |
| today | *hoy* |
| tomorrow | *mañana* |
| day after tomorrow | *pasado mañana* |
| tonight | *esta noche* |
| yesterday | *ayer* |
| day before yesterday | *anteayer* |
| yesterday morning | *ayer por la mañana* |

**units of time**

| | |
|---|---|
| century | *siglo* |
| day | *día* |
| daily | *diario* |
| | *cotidiano* |
| decade | *década* |
| hour | *hora* |
| hourly (per hour) | *por hora* |
| hourly (each hour) | *cada hora* |
| instant | *instante* |
| minute | *minuto* |
| moment | *momento* |
| month | *mes* |
| monthly | *mensual* |

| | |
|---|---|
| monthly (adv) | *mensualmente* |
| second | *segundo* |
| week | *semana* |
| weekly | *semanal* |

**general terms**

| | |
|---|---|
| during | *durante (prep)* |
| event | *evento* |
| frequency | *frecuencia* |
| occasion | *ocasión* |
| occurrence | *ocurrencia* |
| recurrent | *recurrente* |
| time | *tiempo* |

**recurrent events**

| | |
|---|---|
| anniversary | *aniversario* |
| Sabbath | *sábado* |
| | |
| hourly (by the hour) | *por horas (adv)* |
| nowadays | *hoy en dia* |

**Months of the year**

| | |
|---|---|
| January | *enero* |
| February | *febrero* |
| March | *marzo* |
| April | *abril* |
| May | *mayo* |
| June | *junio* |
| July | *julio* |
| August | *agosto* |
| September | *septiembre* |
| October | *octubre* |
| November | *noviembre* |
| December | *diciembre* |

### Inexact Time Units

| | |
|---|---|
| epoch | *época* |
| era | *era* |
| eternity | *eternidad* |
| future | *futuro* |
| instant | *instante* |
| moment | *momento* |
| past | *pasado* |
| pause | *pausa* |
| period | *periodo, período* |
| present | *presente* |

### Time Associations

| | |
|---|---|
| abrupt | *abrupto* |
| brief | *breve* |
| continual, continuous | *continuo* |
| durable | *durable/ duradero* |
| enduring | *duradero* |
| interminable | *interminable* |
| long-lived | *longevo* |
| momentary | *momentáneo* |
| permanent | *permanente* |
| prolonged | *prolongado* |
| provisional | *provisional* |
| temporal | *temporal/ temporario* |
| tentative | *tentativo* |
| transitory | *transitorio* |

### Average

| | |
|---|---|
| acceptable | *aceptable* |
| adequate | *adecuado* |
| general | *general* |
| mediocre | *mediocre* |
| moderate | *moderado* |
| natural | *natural* |

| | |
|---|---|
| normal | *normal* |
| ordinary | *ordinario* |
| reasonable | *razonable* |
| regular | *regular* |
| routine | *rutinario* |
| satisfactory | *satisfactorio* |
| standard | *estándar* |
| typical | *típico* |
| universal | *universal* |
| usual | *usual* |

### Above normal

| | |
|---|---|
| abundant | *abundante* |
| ample | *amplio* |
| appreciable | *apreciable* |
| considerable | *considerable* |
| crucial | *crucial* |
| definitive | *definitivo* |
| dominant, dominating | *dominando/ dominante* |
| enormous | *enorme* |
| excellent | *excelente* |
| excessive | *excesivo* |
| extensive | *extensivo* |
| gigantic | *gigante* |
| grand | *grandioso (a)/ grande* |
| ideal | *ideal* |
| immeasurable | *inmensurable* |
| immense | *inmenso* |
| innumerable | *innumerable* |
| intense | *intenso* |
| magnificent | *magnifico* |
| majestic | *majestuoso* |
| major | *mayor* |
| marvelous | *maravilloso* |
| massive | *masivo* |

| | |
|---|---|
| monumental | *monumental* |
| much | *mucho* |
| necessary | *necesario* |
| overestimate | *sobreestimado* |
| overvalued | *sobrevalorado* |
| precious | *precioso* |
| precise | *preciso* |
| predominant | *predominante* |
| priceless | *inapreciable* |
| principal | *principal* |
| priority | *prioridad* |
| profound | *profundo* |
| profuse | *profuso* |
| prominent | *prominente* |
| remote | *remoto* |
| rich | *rico* |
| severe | *severo* |
| significant | *significativo/ significante* |
| spacious | *espacioso* |
| spectacular | *espectacular* |
| splendid | *espléndido* |
| substantial | *su(b)stancial, su(b)stancioso* |
| sufficient | *suficiente* |
| superior | *superior* |
| tremendous | *tremendo* |
| vast | *vasto* |

### *below normal*

| | |
|---|---|
| concise | *conciso* |
| deficient | *deficiente* |
| diminished | *disminuido* |
| inferior | *inferior* |
| insignificant | *insignificante* |
| insufficient | *insuficiente* |
| mere | *mero (a)* |

| | |
|---|---|
| modest | *modesto* |
| poor | *pobre* |
| reduced | *reducido* |
| scarce | *escaso* |
| superficial | *superficial* |
| unimportant (adj) | *sin importancia* |
| unnecessary | *innecesario* |
| unsatisfactory | *insatisfactorio* |

# Biblical Foods and Useful Food Expressions

| | |
|---|---|
| beef | *carne de res* |
| bread | *pan* |
| break | *cortar/ quebrar* |
| cereal | *cereal* |
| chicken | *pollo* |
| cooked | *cocinado/ cocido* |
| corn | *maíz/ elote* |
| dish | *plato, platillo* |
| dove | *paloma* |
| a drink | *una bebida* |
| fat | *grasa* |
| fish | *pescado* |
| flour | *harina* |
| food | *comida* |
| food allergies | *alergias a la comida* |
| grain | *grano, cereal* |
| internal organs | *organos internos/ órganos intérnales* |
| juice | *jugo* |
| manna | *maná* |
| meat | *carne* |
| milk | *leche* |
| oatmeal | *avena, harina de avena* |
| oat | *avena* |
| pigeon | *paloma* |
| pork | *puerco* |
| prepared | *preparado* |
| raw | *crudo* |
| safe | *seguro* |

| | |
|---|---|
| seafood | *mariscos* |
| unleavened bread | *pan sin levadura* |
| water | *agua* |
| wine | *vino* |
| yeast | *levadura* |

### Parts of animal

| | |
|---|---|
| breast | *pecho* |
| head | *cabeza* |
| intestines | *intestinos* |
| kidney | *riñón* |
| leg | *pierna* |
| liver | *hígado* |
| neck | *cuello* |
| stomach | *estomago* |
| tail | *cola* |
| thigh | *muslo* |

### Preparing food

| | |
|---|---|
| bake | *hornear* |
| boil | *hervir* |
| crop | *cosecha* |
| fry | *freír* |
| medium (doneness) | *termino medio* |
| rare | *crudo* |
| raw | *crudo* |
| roast, roasted meat | *asado, carne asado* |
| simmer | *cocer a fuego lento* |
| slaughter | *matanza* |
| well done | *bien cocido* |

| | |
|---|---|
| vegetarian | *vegetariano* |
| vegan | *vegano* |
| diabetic | *diabético* |

# FASTING

This section contains selections from Elmer T. Towns', Fasting for Spiritual Breakthrough. / *Esta seccion contiene selecciones de Elmer T. Towns', en ayunas*

fasting

*ayuno*

### Purpose of Fasting

to chasten the soul (Ps. 69:10)

*corregir la alma*

to humble yourself (Ez. 8:21; Ps. 35:13)

*ser humilde/ humillarse*

to seek the Lord (2 Chron. 20:3,4)

*Para buscar a Dios/consultar al Señor*

to prepare for spiritual warfare (Matt. 17:21, Joel 1:14, 2:12, Jon. 3: 4,5)

*preparar para guerras espirituales*

During period of national mourning (1 Sam. 31:11–13)

*Durante un periodo de luto nacional*

When concerned for the welfare of others (Ps. 35:13)

*Cuando se preocupa por el bienestar de otros*

When challenged by personal concerns (2 Sam. 12:15–17)

*Cuando tienes dificultades personales*

When facing danger (2 Chron. 20: 2,3; Ezra 8:21–23)

*En situaciones de peligro/ peligrosos*

When engaged in spiritual warfare (Matt. 17:21; Mark 9:29)

*Enfrentarse a un combate espiritual*

When ordaining ministers of the gospel (Acts 13: 2,3; Acts 14:23)

*Cuando ordena ministros para evangelismo*

### Fasting Accompanied by

| | |
|---|---|
| abstinence from sexual relationships (1 Cor. 7:5) | *abstenerse de relaciones sexuales* |
| confession of sin (1 Sam. 7:6; Neh. 9:1–3) | *confesión de pecados* |
| humiliation (Deut. 9:18; Ps. 35:13) | *humillación* |
| lamenting (Esther 9:30,31) | *lamentando* |
| mourning (2 Sam. 1:12; 1 Kings 21:27; Esther 4:3; Neh. 1:4; Joel 2:12; Ezra 10:6) | *luto* |
| personal demeanor (Matt. 6:17) | *conducta personal cuando en ayuno* |
| prayer (Ezra 8:23; Neh. 1:4; Ps. 35:13; Dan. 9:13; Luke 5:33) | *orar* |
| reading the scriptures (Neh. 9:1–3; Jer. 36:6; Jer. 36:10) | *leyendo las escrituras* |
| weeping (2 Sam. 1:12; Neh. 1:4; Esther 4:3, Ps. 69:10; Joel 2:12) | *llanto/llorón* |
| worship (Neh. 1–3) | *alabanza* |

### Promised blessings associated with fasting

| | |
|---|---|
| answered prayer, insight, restoration (Isa. 58:9–12) | oraciones contestadas, sabiduría, restauración |
| joy, gladness, cheerfulness (Zech. 8:19) | *alegría* |
| rewarded by God the Father (Matt. 6: 17,18) | *Premios de Dios El Padre* |
| spiritual power over demons (Matt. 17:21; Mark 9:29) | *Poder espiritual sobre los demonios* |
| spiritual power over demons (Matt. 17:21; Mark 9:29) | *Poderes espirituales sobre los demonios* |

# HEALING AND HEALTH RELATED VOCABULARY AND SIMPLE EXPRESSIONS

This list is in no way intended to be exhaustive nor is it intended to provide medical advice. If you need an exhaustive list of medical terms consult a bilingual medical dictionary or a bilingual vocabulary dictionary.

### Brief Expressions/Sentences

| | |
|---|---|
| I am sick. | *¿Estoy enfermo (a))?* |
| Are you (formal) sick? | *¿Esta enfermo (a)?* |
| Are you (informal) sick? | *¿Estas enfermo (a)?* |
| Where does it hurt? | *¿A donde te duele?* |
| What is your illness? | *¿Cuál es su enfermedad?* |
| Is there a doctor nearby? | *¿Hay un doctor cerca de aquí?* |

### *General sections of the body*

| | |
|---|---|
| abdomen | *abdomen* |
| arms | *brazos* |
| bust | *busto* |
| extremities | *extremidades* |
| head | *cabeza* |
| torso | *torso* |
| trunk | *trunco* |

### *Different parts of the body*

| | |
|---|---|
| blood | *sangre* |
| cell | *célula* |
| ears | *orejas* |

| | |
|---|---|
| eyes | *ojos* |
| feet | *pies* |
| hair | *cabello* |
| hands | *manos* |
| heart | *corazón* |
| knees | *rodillas* |
| legs | *piernas* |
| mind | *mente* |
| muscles | *músculos* |
| nerves | *nervios* |
| teeth | *dientes* |
| throat | *garganta* |
| tissue | *tejido* |
| toes | *dedos* |
| tongue | *lengua* |

### Types of sicknesses

| | |
|---|---|
| fever | *fiebre* |
| headache | *dolor de cabeza* |
| leprosy | *lepra* |
| listlessness | *falta de interés* |
| cancer | *cáncer* |
| AIDS | *SIDA* |
| appetite | *apetito* |
| period (menstrual) | *periodo menstrual* |
| cholesterol | *colesterol* |
| diabetes | *diabetes* |
| heart attack | *ataque cardiaco* |
| nauseous | *nausea* |
| vomit | *vomito* |
| pregnancy | *embarazo* |
| pregnant | *embarazado* |
| operation | *operación* |
| coma | *coma* |
| remedy | *remedio* |

| | |
|---|---|
| symptom | *síntoma* |
| infection | *infección* |
| influenza | *influenza* |
| abscess | *absceso* |
| pneumonia | *neumonía* |
| rheumatism | *reumatismo* |
| tetanus | *tétano(s)* |

## *Medical practitioners and places*

| | |
|---|---|
| doctor | *doctor* |
| medicine | *medicina* |
| medical | *medico* |
| nurse | *enfermera* |
| clinic | *clínica* |
| hospital | *hospital* |
| healer | *curandero, médico* |

# Frequently Mentioned Biblical Animal, Animal Related Words, and other Useful Animals

| | |
|---|---|
| animal | *animal* |
| beast | *bestia* |
| cat | *gato* |
| creature | *criatura* |
| dog | *perro* |
| donkey | *burro, -a* |
| eagle | *águila* |
| elephant | *elefante* |
| falcon | *halcón* |
| fish | *pez* |
| horse | *caballo* |
| iguana | *iguana* |
| lion | *león* |
| lioness | *leona* |
| mosquito | *mosquito* |
| mule | *mulo, -a* |
| rat | *rata* |
| serpent | *serpiente, sierpe (poetic)* |
| tiger | *tigre* |
| tigress | *tigresa* |
| tortoise | *tortuga* |
| turtle | *tortuga* |
| sheep | *ovejas* |
| goat | *cabra* |

| donkey | *burro, asno* |
| lamb | *cordero* |

### Groups of Animals

| herd | *manada, rebaño* |
| flock | *multitud, bandada* |
| bite | *mordedura, bocado, picadura* |
| dangerous | *peligroso* |
| domestic | *domestico* |
| tame | *domestico* |
| wild | *salvaje* |

# Sins

| | |
|---|---|
| adulterer | *adultero (m) –ra (f)* |
| adultery | *adulterio* |
| arrogance | *arrogancia* |
| bearing false | *testigo falso* |
| bribe | *soborno* |
| bribery | *soborno* |
| cheating | *tramposo (-a)* |
| corruption | *corrupción* |
| evil | *malvado* |
| fear | *miedo* |
| gluttony | *glotonería* |
| ill gotten | *mal conseguido* |
| laziness | *pereza* |
| lying | *mentiroso (sa)* |
| mockery | *burlarse; fingido* |
| offense | *ofensa* |
| pay back | *devolver, reembolsar* |
| perverse | *perverso (sa)* |
| perversion | *tergiversación, perversión sexual* |
| root of all evil | *raíz de todos los males* |
| scoundrel | *sinvergüenza, canalla* |
| sin of Ada**m** | *pecado de Adán* |
| sloth | *pereza* |
| stealing | *robando* |
| to cheat | *engañar, timar* |
| unforgivable sin | *pecado imperdonable* |
| worry | *preocupación/inquietud* |

## Other Sin Vocabulary

| | |
|---|---|
| to forgive | *perdonar, disculpar* |
| willingness to forgive | *compasión* |
| forgiveness | *perdón* |
| turn away | *echar, alejar* |
| unforgiveness | *no perdonar* |
| heart | *corazón* |
| iniquities | *iniquidades* |
| reject | *echar* |
| cleanse | *limpiar* |
| (don't do it again) renounce | *renunciar* |
| repent | *arrepentirse* |
| repentant | *arrepentido* |
| repentance | *arrepentimiento* |
| unrepentant | *impenitente* |

# WEATHER RELATED
# BIBLICAL TERMS

| | |
|---|---|
| storm | *tormenta, tempestad* |
| clouds | *nubes* |
| rainbow | *arcoíris* |
| rain | *lluvia* |
| drought | *sequía* |
| disaster | *desastre* |
| tornado | *tornado* |
| hurricane | *huracán* |
| wind | *viento* |
| windy | *ventoso* |
| cloudy | *nublado* |
| snow | *nieve* |

# Attitudes/Feelings/ Emotions

| | |
|---|---|
| abandonment | *abandono* |
| affection | *cariño* |
| agree | *estar de acuerdo* |
| anger | *enojo* |
| anxiety | *ansioso* |
| | *inquieto* |
| | *asegurar* |
| attitude | *actitud* |
| to be able to | *ser capaz de* |
| complain | *quejarse* |
| complaint | *queja* |
| confusion | *confusión* |
| cry | *llorar* |
| crying | *llanto* |
| depressed | *deprimido* |
| depression | *depresión* |
| desperate | *desesperado* |
| despair, desperation | *desesperación* |
| disagree | *no estar de acuerdo* |
| disagreement | *desacuerdo* |
| be against | *estar en contra de* |
| discontent | *descontento* |
| discouraged | *desanimado* |
| dissatisfaction | *descontento* |
| dissatisfied | *descontento* |
| encourage | *animar a alguien* |
| | *estimular* |
| enthusiasm | *entusiasmo* |

| | |
|---|---|
| faith, trust | *fe* |
| | *confianza* |
| trust | *tener confianza* |
| feel | *sentirse* |
| feel like | *tener ganas de* |
| fun, enjoyment | *alegría* |
| | *diversión* |
| have fun | *divertirse* |
| gratitude | *gratitud* |
| happiness | *felicidad* |
| happy | *feliz* |
| | *contento* |
| have to | *tener que* |
| hope (v) | *esperar* |
| hope (n) | *esperanza* |
| indifference | *indiferencia* |
| indifferent | *indiferente* |
| joy | *alegría* |
| jealous | *celoso* |
| laugh | *reír* |
| laughter | *risa* |
| matter | *importar* |
| humor | *humor* |
| bad mood | *mal humor* |
| good mood | *buen humor* |
| need | *necesitar* |
| need | *necesidad* |
| patience | *paciencia* |
| have patience | *tener paciencia* |
| pleasure | *placer* |
| relief | *alivio* |
| relieve | *aliviar* |
| sad | *triste* |
| sadness | *tristeza* |
| to become sad | *entristecerse* |

| | |
|---|---|
| satisfaction | *satisfacción* |
| satisfied | *satisfecho* |
| selfish | *egoísta* |
| shame | *vergüenza* |
| be ashamed | *tener vergüenza* |
| smile | *sonreír* |
| smile | *sonrisa* |
| sorrow | *dolor* |
| | *pena* |
| surprise | *sorpresa* |
| sympathy (over a death) | *pésame* |
| | *condolencia* |
| sympathetic | *compasivo* |
| thankfulness | *agradecimiento* |
| thankful | *agradecido* |
| thank | *agradecer* |
| want to | *querer* |

# PLACES

| | |
|---|---|
| abbey | *la abadía* |
| abbey | *abadía* |
| altar | *altar* |
| baptistery, baptistery | *baptisterio, bautisterio* |
| cathedral | *la catedral* |
| chapel | *capilla* |
| church | *la iglesia* |
| cloister | *claustro* |
| confessional | *confesionario* |
| convent | *convento* |
| convent | *convento* |
| Holy City | *La Ciudad Sancta* |
| Holy Land | *Tierra Santo* |
| Holy Roman Empire | *El Sacro Imperio Romano* |
| mission | *misión* |
| monastery | *monasterio* |
| mosque | *la mezquita* |
| pagoda | *pagoda* |
| paradise | *paraíso* |
| priory | *priorato* |
| sacristy | *sacristía* |
| sanctuary | *santuario* |
| synagogue | *la sinagoga* |
| temple | *el templo* |

### holy cities

| | |
|---|---|
| Bethlehem | *Belén* |
| Jerusalem | *Jerusalén* |
| Mecca | *Meca* |
| Rome | *Roma* |
| Zion (obs) | *Sión* |

# Christian Church Events

| | |
|---|---|
| anniversary | *aniversario* |
| baptism | *bautizmo* |
| benediction | *bendición* |
| birth | *nacimiento* |
| birthday | *cumpleaños* |
| camp meeting | |
| christening | *bautizo* |
| collection/offering | *ofrenda* |
| communion | *comunión* |
| concert | *concierto* |
| conference | *conferencia* |
| confirmation | *confirmación* |
| consecration | *consagración* |
| death | *muerto* |
| devotion | *devoción* |
| funeral | *funeral* |
| invitation to Christ | *invitación a Jesucristo* |
| meeting | *junta* |
| open the doors of the church | *abre las puertas de la iglesia* |
| prayer meeting | |
| retreat | *retiro* |
| revival | *renacimiento ?* |
| Sunday School | |

# Clothing and Materials Related to Religious Practice

| | |
|---|---|
| christening gown | *bautismal* |
| habit (nuns wear) | *hábito* |
| robe | *túnica* |
| tunic | *túnica* |
| turban | *turbante* |
| ephod | *el efod* |
| cross | *cruz* |

# OLD TESTAMENT
# RITUAL MATERIALS

| | |
|---|---|
| incense | *incienso* |
| utensils | *utensilios* |
| temple | *templo* |
| blood | *sangre* |
| burn | *quemar* |
| sacrifice | *sacrificio* |
| offer | *ofrecer* |

# METALS AND MINERALS MENTIONED IN THE BIBLE

adamant (diamond) Jer 17:1
agate Exod. 28:19
alabaster                        *mármol/alabastro*
amethyst Rev 21:20               *amatista*
beryl Exod. 28:20                *berilio*
brass                            *latón*
brimstone                        *azufre*
bronze                           *bronce*
copper                           *cobre*
crystal (quartz)                 *cristal*
diamond Exod 28:18               *diamante*
emerald                          *esmeralda*
gold      oro                    *oro*
iron                             *hierro*
jacinth                          *Jacinto*
jasper                           *jaspe*
lapis                            *lapis lazuli*
lead                             *plomo*
onyx                             *ónix*
pearl                            *perla*
ruby                             *rubí*
salt                             *sal*
sapphire                         *zafiro*
silver    plata                  *plata*
soda                             *carbonato de sodio*
tin                              *lata, latón*
topaz                            *topacio*
turquoise                        *turquesa*

# Types of Religions
# and Doctrines

## Types of Religions
| | |
|---|---|
| animism | *Animismo* |
| atheism | *Ateísmo* |
| demonism | *Demonismo* |
| pantheism | *Panteísmo* |
| polytheism | *Politeísmo* |

## Doctrines
| | |
|---|---|
| agnosticism | *Agnosticismo* |
| anabaptism | *Anabaptismo* |
| anabaptism | *Anabaptismo* |
| apologetics | *Apologética* |
| asceticism | *Ascetismo* |
| caste | *casta* |
| celibacy | *celibato* |
| clericalism | *clericalismo* |
| deism | *deísmo* |
| dispensation | *dispensa* |
| dogma | *dogma* |
| dualism | *dualismo* |
| ecumenism | *ecumenismo* |
| ethics | *ética* |
| evangelism | *evangelismo* |
| fetishism | *fetichismo* |
| fundamentalism | *fundamentalismo* |
| Gnosticism | *(g)nosticismo* |
| heterodoxy | *heterodoxia* |
| humanism | *humanismo* |

| | |
|---|---|
| karma | *karma* |
| messianism | *mesianismo* |
| monasticism | *monaquismo, monacato* |
| mosaic law | *ley mosaica* |
| mysticism | *misticismo* |
| omnipotence | *omnipotencia* |
| orthodoxy | *ortodoxia* |
| paganism | *paganismo* |
| Pietism | *pietismo* |
| ritualism | *ritualismo* |
| Satanism | *satanismo* |
| schism | *cisma* |
| scholasticism | *escolasticismo* |
| sectarianism | *sectarismo* |
| secularism | *secularismo* |
| spiritism | *espiritismo* |
| spiritualism | *espiritualismo* |
| syncretism | *sincretismo* |
| theocracy | *teocracia* |
| theosophy | *teosofía* |

# Parts of a Church

| | |
|---|---|
| aisle | *pasillo* |
| pulpit | *pulpito* |
| altar | *altar* |
| pew | *banco de iglesia* |
| nave | *almacen, nave* |
| steeple | *aguja, campanario* |
| porch | *pórtico* |
| churchyard | *cementerio, camposanto* |
| door | *puerta* |

# HOLY PLACES

| | |
|---|---|
| abbey | *abadía* |
| altar | *altar* |
| baptistery, baptistery | *baptisterio, bautisterio* |
| cathedral | *catedral* |
| chapel | *capilla* |
| cloister | *claustro* |
| confessional | *confesionario* |
| convent | *convento* |
| mission | *misión* |
| monastery | *monasterio* |
| mosque | *mezquita* |
| pagoda | *pagoda* |
| paradise | *paraíso* |
| priory | *priorato* |
| sacristy | *sacristía* |
| sanctuary | *santuario* |
| synagogue | *sinagoga* |
| temple | *templo* |

# PEOPLE

| | |
|---|---|
| agnostic | *agnóstico* |
| anointed person | *ungido* |
| atheist | *ateo* |
| believer | *creyente* |
| catholic | *católico/a* |
| clergy | *clero* |
| clergyman | *clérigo* |
| congregation | *congregación, feligreses* |
| human | *humano* |
| human being | *ser humano* |
| minister | *pastor (Protestant English Christian)* |
| monk | *el monje* |
| pagan | *pagano* |
| pope | *el papa* |
| practicing | *practicante* |
| priest | *cura* |
| priesthood | *el sacerdocio* |
| protestant | *protestante* |
| religious | *religioso/a* |

### *Religious Titles*

| | |
|---|---|
| abbess | *abadesa* |
| abbot | *abad* |
| archbishop | *arzobispo* |
| archdeacon | *archidiácono* |
| bishop | *obispo* |
| chaplain | *capellán* |
| Dalai Lama | *Dalai Lama* |
| deacon | *diácono* |

| | |
|---|---|
| deaconess | *diaconisa* |
| friar | *fraile* |
| imam | *imán* |
| lama | *lama* |
| mahatma | *mahatma* |
| metropolitan | *metropolitano* |
| ordinary | *ordinario* |
| pastor | *pastor* |
| pontiff | *pontífice* |
| Pope | *papa* |
| prelate | *prelado* |
| primate | *primado* |
| prior | *prior* |
| prioress | *priora* |
| rabbi | *rabí, rabino* |
| rector | *rector* |
| reverend | *reverendo* |
| vicar | *vicario, párroco* |

### *groups*

| | |
|---|---|
| clergy | *clero* |
| congregation | *congregación* |
| denomination | *denominación* |
| laity | *laicado* |
| sect | *secta* |

### *scholars*

| | |
|---|---|
| seminarian | *seminarista* |
| Talmudist | *talmudista* |
| theologian | *teólogo* |

### *special purpose practitioners*

| | |
|---|---|
| baptizer | *bautista* |
| cantor | *cantor(a)* |

| | |
|---|---|
| clergyman | *clérigo* |
| clergywoman | *clériga* |
| cleric | *clérigo, -a* |
| confessor | *confesor(a)* |
| curate | *cura* |
| ecclesiastic | *eclesiástico, -a* |
| evangelist | *evangelista, evangelizador(a)* |
| exorcist | *exorcista* |
| guardian | *guardián, -ana* |
| lector | *rabino* |
| legate | *legado* |
| liturgist | *liturgista* |
| minister | *ministro, -a* |
| missionary | *misionero, -a* |
| monk | *monje* |
| officiate | *oficiante* |
| patron saint | *patrono, -a* |
| prophet | *profeta* |
| psalmist | *salmista* |
| rabbi | *rabino* |

# CONNECTORS

| | |
|---|---|
| more than ever | *mas que nunca* |
| always | *siempre* |
| never | *nunca* |

# JOBS IN THE CHURCH

| | |
|---|---|
| altar boy | *monaguillo (iglesia católica)* |
| choir director | *director del coro* |
| choir member | *miembro del coro* |
| deacon | *diácono* |
| first lady | *primera dama* |
| janitor | *portero (a)* |
| laymen | *seglar, lego* |
| leader | *líder* |
| pastor | *pastor* |
| praise and worship dancers | *alabanza y danzadoras de alabanza* |
| praise team | *equipo de alabanza* |
| priest | *sacerdote* |
| rabbi | *rabí* |
| secretary | *secretaria* |
| soloist | *solista* |
| teacher | *maestro (, -a)* |
| usher | *acomodador* |

# SACRED

| | |
|---|---|
| holy | *sagrado, santo* |
| holiness | *santidad* |
| sacred | *sagrado* |
| to hold something sacred | *considerar algo sagrado* |
| divine | *divino* |
| divinely | *divinamente* |
| pious | *pio, piadoso, beato* |
| piety | *piedad* |

# BIBLICAL VERBS AND RELATED NOUNS

| | |
|---|---|
| to explain | *explicar* |
| the explanation | *la explicación* |
| to compare | *comparar* |
| the comparison | *la comparación* |
| to minister | *atender* |
| the minister | *ministrar, atender* |
| the ministry | *ministerio* |
| to praise | *alabar* |
| the praise | *alabanza* |
| to worship | *adorar* |
| to honor | *honrar* |
| the honor | *el honor* |
| to obey | *obedecer* |
| in obediente | *en obediencia a* |
| to love | *amar* |
| the love | *el amor* |
| to heal | *curar* |
| the health | *la salud* |
| to encourage | *animar a alguien* |
| to bless | *bendecir* |
| the blessing | *la bendición* |
| to pray | *orar, rezar* |
| the prayer | *la oración* |
| to succeed | *triunfar, tener éxito* |
| to sing | *cantar* |
| the song | *la canción* |
| to sin | *pecar* |
| to cover | *cubrir* |

# Wisdom and Knowledge

| | |
|---|---|
| adoration | *adoración* |
| discipline | *disciplina* |
| evil | *la maldad* |
| faith | *fe* |
| faithful | *fiel* |
| godliness | *devoción* |
| good | *el bueno* |
| intelligence | *inteligencia* |
| interpretation | *interpretación* |
| knowledge | *conocimiento* |
| obedience | *obediencia, ser obediente* |
| power | *poder* |
| right | *correcto* |
| understanding | *entendimiento* |
| wisdom | *sabiduría* |
| wrong | *falso, equivocado* |

# BIBLICAL BLESSINGS

| | |
|---|---|
| blessings of Abraham | *bendiciones de Abraham* |
| discernment | *entendimiento, discernimiento* |
| health | *salud* |
| peace | *paz* |
| power | *poder* |
| protection | *protección* |
| spiritual riches | *riquezas espirituales* |
| strength | *fuerza* |
| to be kept | *para ser guardado* |
| wealth | *riqueza* |
| wisdom | *sabiduría* |

# BIBLICAL WARFARE
# (DELIVERANCE)

**abolish**                     *abolir*
to end                          *terminar*
to cut                          *cortar*
to strike through               *ataque a través*

**beat down**                   *vencer*
to beat                         *golpear*
to bruise                       *magullar, contusionar*
to violently strike             *ataque violento, o con violencia*
to crush                        *aplastar*
to destroy                      *arruinar (life), destruir (building)*
to discomfort                   *incomodidad (lack of comfort)*
to break through by violence    *abrirse paso con violencia,*
                                *penetrar en las defensas enemigas*
to dismay                       *consternación*
to penetrate                    *penetrar*
to terrify                      *aterrorizar*

**break down**                  *echar abajo*
to deliver                      *llevar, cumplir*
to break                        *quebrar, romperse*
to render something useless     *hacer que algo resulta inútil*
to crush                        *aplastar*
to destroy                      *destruir*

| | |
|---|---|
| **to spoil (by breaking into pieces)** | ***estropear (quebrandose en pedazos)*** |
| to pluck down | *tirón abajo* |
| to pull down | *derribar* |
| to ruin | *arruinar, destruir* |
| to beat down | *acabar con, golpear, vencer* |
| to cast down | *derribar* |
| to dash in pieces | *lanzarse en pedazos* |
| to disperse | *dispersar* |
| to tear down | *tirar, demoler, derribar* |
| to break down | *romperse, quebrarse* |
| to destroy | *destruir* |
| to overthrow | *deroccar* |
| to pull down | *echar abajo* |
| to throw down | *echar abajo* |
| to cast down to hell | *echar al infierno* |
| | |
| **cast out** | ***arrojar*** |
| to seize | *aprovechar* |
| to rob | *robar* |
| to inherit | *heredar* |
| to expel | *expulsar, echar* |
| impoverished | *empobrecido(a)* |
| to send away | *despedir, despachar* |
| to push away or down | *rechazar* |
| to cast away | *naufragar* |
| to banish | *desaparecer, expulsar, desterrar, apartar de* |
| to eject | *expulsar* |
| to send out | *mandar salir, echar fuera* |
| to throw out | *tirar, botar (trash, rubbish)* |

| | |
|---|---|
| **chase (pursue)** | *perseguir* |
| put to flight | *hicieron huir* |
| persecute | *perseguir* |
| | |
| **confound (confuse)** | *confundir (confuso)* |
| to be ashamed | *tener vergüenza* |
| to be disappointed | *desilusionado* |
| brought to confusion | *desorientación* |
| put to shame | *humillar* |
| | |
| **consume** | *consumir* |
| to end | *terminar* |
| consume away | *consumir* |
| destroy | *destruir* |
| make clean riddance | *liberación, ser limpio* |
| to eat up | *consumir* |
| devour | *devorar* |
| burn up | *quemar, consumirse* |
| | |
| **contend** | *contender* |
| to grate | *rechinar* |
| to anger | *enojar* |
| to meddle | *entrometerse* |
| to strive | *esforzarse, procurar, luchar por* |
| to strive for, to strive after | *esforzarse por conseguir algo* |
| to stir up | *provocar, excitar* |
| to grapple with | *luchar con* |
| to defend | *defender* |
| to chide | *reprender* |
| to rebuke | *reprender, reprochar* |
| initiate a controversy | *iniciar una controversia* |

| | |
|---|---|
| **destroy** | *destruir* |
| to end | *terminar* |
| to cease | *cesar, acabar* |
| destroy utterly | *destruir absolutamente* |
| make clean | *hacerse limpio, limpiar* |
| waste | *desperdicio* |
| make accursed | *hacer maldito* |
| tear down | *destruir* |
| break down | *romper, derribar* |
| to devour | *devorar* |
| to eat up | *consumir* |
| | |
| **fight** | *pelear* |
| to consume | *consumir* |
| to battle | *a la batalla, luchar* |
| to make war | *hacer guerra* |
| overcome | *vencer, superar* |
| prevail | *prevalecer* |
| struggle | *luchar* |
| contend with the adversary | *lluchar contra adversario* |
| | *contender con enemigo* |
| | *competir con adversario* |
| | |
| **prevail** | *prevalecer* |
| to enclose | *encerrar* |
| to hold back | *retener, retrasar* |
| to shut up | *callar (silence)* |
| stop | *parar* |
| be strong | *sea fuerte* |
| put on strength | *Adoptar una postura de valor/fuerza* |
| to overpower | *predominar* |
| to restrain | *refrenar* |
| bind | *ligar* |
| conquer | *conquistar* |

| **smite** | **herir** |
| --- | --- |
| to strike | *golpear* |
| to beat | *pegar* |
| cast forth | *expulsar* |
| slaughter | *matanza* |
| give stripes | *pintar una raya/poner limites* |
| wound | *herida* |
| slay | *matar* |
| push | *empujar* |
| defeat | *derrota* |
| inflict | *infligir* |
| dash | *lanzar violentamente* |
| gore | *cornear* |
| hurt | *lastimar* |

| **wrestle** | **luchar** |
| --- | --- |
| to struggle | *lucha (n), pelea (n)* |
| grapple | *enfrentar* |

\* List of words from *Prayers that Rout Demons: Prayers for Defeating Demons and Overthrowing the Power of Darkness* by John Eckhardt (2008). Lake Mary, FL: Charisma Press.

# GENERAL RELIGIOUS TERMS

| | |
|---|---|
| adoration | *adoración* |
| celebration | *celebración* |
| ceremony | *ceremonia* |
| charity | *caridad* |
| conscience | *consciencia* |
| credo, creed | *credo* |
| cult | *culto* |
| deity | *deidad* |
| dissent | *disentir* |
| divinity | *divinidad* |
| doctrine | *doctrina* |
| ecstasy | *éxtasis* |
| ex cathedra | *ex cátedra* |
| faith | *fe* |
| glory | *gloria* |
| intolerance | *intolerancia* |
| martyrdom | *martirio* |
| morality | *moralidad* |
| mystery | *misterio* |
| observance | *observancia* |
| pardon | *perdón* |
| religion | *religión* |
| rite | *rito* |
| ritual | *ritual* |
| sacred | *sagrado, sacro* |
| spiritual | *espiritual* |
| supernatural | *sobrenatural* |
| theology | *teología* |
| tithe | *diezmo* |

| _beliefs_ | _creencias_ |
|---|---|
| Assumption | _Suposición_ |
| destiny | _destino_ |
| exoneration | _exoneración_ |
| expiation | _expiación_ |
| immanence, immanency | _inmanencia_ |
| immortality | _inmortalidad_ |
| incarnation | _encarnación_ |
| inferno | _infierno_ |
| limbo | _limbo_ |
| miracle | _milagro_ |
| nirvana | _nirvana_ |
| perdition | _perdición_ |
| possession | _posesión_ |
| predestination | _predestinación_ |
| providence | _providencia_ |
| purgatory | _purgatorio_ |
| redemption | _redención_ |
| reincarnation | _reencarnación_ |
| resurrection | _resurrección_ |
| salvation | _salvación_ |
| sanctity | _santidad_ |
| savior | _salvador (a)_ |
| superstition | _superstición_ |
| theism | _teísmo_ |
| transcendence | _transcendencia_ |
| transfiguration | _transfiguración_ |
| transmigration | _transmigración_ |
| transubstantiation | _transubstanciación_ |
| trinity | _trinidad_ |

| **prediction in religion** | **predicción en religión** |
| --- | --- |
| preordination | *preordinación* |
| prophecy | *profecía* |
| revelation | *revelación* |
| sign | *señal* |

# ORGANIZATIONS AND OFFICES

| | |
|---|---|
| archdiocese | *archidiócesis, arquidiócesis* |
| benefice | *beneficio* |
| bishopric | *obispado* |
| college | *colegio* |
| consistory | *consistorio* |
| deaconry | *diaconado, diaconato* |
| diocese | *diócesis* |
| episcopate | *episcopado* |
| order | *orden* |
| papacy, popedom | *papado* |
| parish | *parroquia* |
| prelacy | *prelacía* |
| rabbinate | *rabinato* |
| synod | *sínodo* |
| Vatican | *Vaticano* |
| vicarage | *vicaría* |

| **scholarship and translation** | ***beca y traducción*** |
|---|---|
| alteration | *alteración* |
| concordance | *concordancia* |
| demonology | *demonología* |
| emendation | *enmienda* |
| eschatology | *escatología* |
| index | *índice* |
| seminary | *seminario* |
| yeshiva | *yeshivá* |

| **other terms** | **otros terminos** |
|---|---|
| apostasy | *apostasía* |
| celestial | *celestial* |
| devout | *devoto* |
| interdict, interdiction | *interdicto* |
| octave | *octava* |
| omniscient | *omnisciente* |
| practice | *practicar* |
| prebend | *prebenda* |
| temporal | *temporal* |

# NAMES

| | |
|---|---|
| *founders of religions* | *de fundadores de religiones* |
| Abraham | *Abrahán* |
| Christ | *Cristo* |
| Jesus Christ | *Jesucristo* |
| Luther | *Lutero* |
| Mohammed, Muhammad | *Mahoma* |
| Moses | *Moisés* |

| | |
|---|---|
| *major world religions* | *principales religiones del mundo* |
| Buddhism | *budismo* |
| Christianity | *cristiandad* |
| Confucianism | *confucianismo* |
| Hinduism | *hinduismo* |
| Islam | *Islam* |
| Judaism | *judaísmo* |
| Shinto | *sintoísmo* |
| Taoism | *taoísmo* |

| | |
|---|---|
| *Other religions and Groups* | *otras religiones y groupos* |
| Anglicanism | *anglicanismo* |
| Bahaism | *bahaísmo* |
| Brahmanism | *brahmanismo* |
| Calvanism | *calvinismo* |
| Catholicism | *catolicismo* |
| Congregationalism | *congregationalismo* |
| Lutheranism | *luteranismo* |
| Methodism | *metodismo* |
| Mormonism | *mormonismo* |

| Orthodox Church | *Iglesia Ortodoxa* |
| Protestantism | *protestantismo* |
| Quakerism | *cuaquerismo* |
| Unification Church | *Iglesia de la Unificación* |
| Unitarianism | *unitarismo* |
| Voodoo | *vudú* |
| Zoroastrianism | *zoroastrismo* |

### deities / diedades

| Allah | *Alá* |
| Brahma | *Brahma* |
| Creator | *Creador* |
| Jehovah | *Jehová* |
| Messiah | *Mesías* |
| Redeemer | *Redentor* |

### sacred books

| Bible | *Biblia* |
| Koran | *Corán* |
| Talmud | *Talmud* |
| Tora | *Tora* |

### holidays and celebrations / fiestas y celebraciones

| Advent | *Adviento* |
| Chanukah, Hanukkah | *Janucá* |
| Epiphany | *Epifanía* |
| Pentecost | *Pentecostés* |
| Purim | *Purim* |
| Ramadan | *Ramadán* |
| Yom Kippur | *Yom Kippur* |

# Practices and Traditions

| | |
|---|---|
| **rites and ceremonies** | *ritos y ceremonias* |
| ablutions | *ablución* |
| absolution | *absolución* |
| baptism | *bautismo, bautizo* |
| bar mitzvah | *bar mitzvah* |
| bat mitzvah | *bat mitzvah* |
| beatification | *beatificación* |
| canonization | *canonización* |
| catechism | *catecismo* |
| circumcision | *circuncisión* |
| communion | *comunión* |
| confession | *confesión* |
| confirmation | *confirmación* |
| consecration | *consagración* |
| contemplation | *contemplación* |
| conversion | *conversión* |
| deification | *deificación* |
| excommunication | *excomunión* |
| exorcism | *exorcismo* |
| festival | *festival* |
| funeral | *funeral* |
| genuflection | *genuflexión* |
| glorification | *glorificación* |
| idolatry | *idolatría* |
| indulgence | *indulgencia* |
| invocation | *invocación* |
| jubilee | *jubileo* |
| liturgy | *liturgia* |
| mass | *misa* |

| meditation | *meditación* |
| occultism | *ocultismo* |
| offering | *ofrenda* |
| Offertory | *ofertorio* |
| ordination | *ordenación* |
| penitence | *penitencia* |
| procession | *procesión* |
| propitiation | *propiciación* |
| purification | *purificación* |
| repentance | *arrepentimiento* |
| response | *respuesta* |
| Sabbath | *sábado* |
| sacrament | *sacramento* |
| sacrifice | *sacrificio* |
| sanctification | *santificación* |
| service | *servicio* |
| supplication | *súplica, suplicación* |
| vespers | *vísperas* |

### eating and drinking — *comiendo y bebiendo*

| abstinence | *abstinencia* |
| dietary (laws) | *dietético, dietético (leyes)* |
| feast | *banquete, fiesta* |
| kosher | *kosher* |
| libation | *libación* |
| renunciation | *renunciación* |
| Seder | *seder* |
| vegetarianism | *vegetarianismo* |

### birth and death

| cremation | *cremación* |
| extreme unction | *extremaunción* |
| reliquary | *relicario* |
| vigil | *vigilia* |

| **objects, charms, symbols** | ***objetos, encantos, y símbolos*** |
|---|---|
| chalice | *cáliz* |
| cross | *cruz* |
| crucifix | *crucifijo* |
| Eucharist | *eucaristía* |
| Host | *hostia* |
| hyssop (obs) | *hisopo* |
| idol | *ídolo* |
| incense | *incienso* |
| menorah | *menorá* |
| oblation | *oblación* |
| rosary | *rosario* |
| tabernacle (on altar) | *tabernáculo* |

| ***sins and crimes*** | ***pecados y crimenes*** |
|---|---|
| anathema | *anatema* |
| blasphemy | *blasfemia* |
| corruption | *corrupción* |
| dissension | *disensión* |
| heresy | *herejía* |
| homosexuality | *homosexualidad* |
| impenitence | *impenitencia* |
| impiety | *impiedad* |
| impurity | *impureza* |
| infidelity | *infidelidad* |
| lust | *lujuria* |
| nonobservance | *incumplimiento* |
| offense | *ofensa* |
| quarrelling | *disputas* |
| sacrilege | *sacrilegio* |
| selfish ambition | *ambición, egoísmo* |
| sodomy | *sodomía* |
| temptation | *tentación* |
| wild parties | *fiestas salvajes* |

## prayers

| | |
|---|---|
| amen | *amén* |
| benediction | *bendición* |
| breviary | *breviario* |
| grace | *gracia* |
| Hallelujah | *aleluya* |
| litany | *letanía* |
| mantra | *mantra* |
| paternoster | *paternóster* |

## literary terms / *términos literarios*

| | |
|---|---|
| allegory | *alegoría* |
| homily | *homilía* |
| parable | *parábola* |
| scripture | *escritura* |
| sermon | *sermón* |

## music and art / *música y arte*

| | |
|---|---|
| canon | *canon* |
| chant | *canto* |
| choir | *coro* |
| Gregorian (chant | *gregoriano* |
| halo | *halo* |
| hymn | *himno* |
| hymnal | *himnario* |
| Kurie | *kirie* |
| Madonna | *Madona* |
| oratorio | *oratorio* |
| passion | *pasión* |
| psalm | *salmo* |
| psalmody | *salmodia* |
| recessional | *himno recesional* |

| supernatural beings | seres sobrenaturales |
| --- | --- |
| angel | *ángel* |
| cherum | *querubín* |
| Christ | *Cristo* |
| Creator | *Creador* |
| demon | *demonio* |
| devil | *diablo* |
| seraph | *serafín* |
| spirit | *espíritu* |

# MEMBERS OF RELIGIOUS GROUPS

### larger groups

| | |
|---|---|
| Bahai | *bahai* |
| Buddhist | *budista* |
| Catholic | *católico, -a* |
| Christian | *cristiano, -a* |
| Hindu | *hindú* |
| Islamite | *islamita* |
| Jew | *judío, -a* |
| Moslem, Muslim | *musulmán, -ana* |
| Protestant | *protestante* |

### Protestants

| | |
|---|---|
| Adventist | *adventista* |
| Anabaptist | *anabaptista* |
| Anglica | *anglicano, -a* |
| Baptist | *bautista* |
| Calvinist | *calvinista* |
| Congregationalist | *congregacionalista* |
| Coptic | *copto, -a* |
| Episcopalian | *episcopalista* |
| Huguenot (obs) | *hugonote* |
| Lutheran | *luterano, -a* |
| Mennonite | *menonita* |
| Methodist | *metodista* |
| Pentecostal | *Pentecostal* |
| Presbyterian | *presbiteriano, -a* |
| Puritan (obs) | *puritano, -a* |
| Quaker | *cuáquero, -a* |

### Jews

| | |
|---|---|
| Ashkenazi | *askenazi* |
| Conservative | *conservador(a)* |
| Hasidism | *hasidismo, jasidismo* |
| Orthodox | *ortodoxo* |
| Reconstructionist | *reconstruccionista* |
| Reform, Reformed | *reformado* |
| Sephardic | *sefardí, sefardita* |

### Muslims

| | |
|---|---|
| Hezbollah | *hezbolá* |
| mujaheddin, mujahedeen | *mujahedeein, mujyaheidin, muyahidín* |
| Shiite | *chiíta, shií* |
| Sufi | *sufí* |
| Sunni | *Suní, sunita* |

### Catholic orders

| | |
|---|---|
| Augustinian | *agustino, -a* |
| Benedictine | *benedictino* |
| Capuchin | *capuchino* |
| Carmelite | *carmelita* |
| Dominican | *dominico* |
| Franciscan | *franciscano* |
| Jacobin | *jacobino* |
| Jesuit | *jesuita* |
| Trappist | *trapense* |

# HISTORICAL TERMS

### persecution against Jews

| | |
|---|---|
| anti-Semitism | *antisemitismo* |
| Diaspora | *diáspora* |
| ghetto | *gueto, ghetto* |
| Holocaust | *Holocausto* |
| Inquisition | *Inquisición* |
| pogrom | *pogromo* |

### other terms

| | |
|---|---|
| Counter-reformation | *Contrarreforma* |
| Crusade | *cruzada* |
| Puritanism (obs) | *puritanismo* |
| Reformation | *Reforma* |

# DEATH

| | |
|---|---|
| cause | *causa* |
| comfort | *confortar* |
| condolence | *condolencia* |
| console | *consolar* |
| fatal | *fatal* |
| inter | *enterrar* |
| lethal | *letal* |
| perish | *perecer* |

### religious aspects

| | |
|---|---|
| cortege, cortège | *cortejo* |
| cremation | *cremación* |
| eternity | *eternidad* |
| funeral | *funeral* |
| immortality | *inmortalidad* |
| resurrection | *resurrección* |

### places

| | |
|---|---|
| cemetery | *cementerio* |
| crematorium, crematory | *crematorio* |
| crypt | *cripta* |
| funeral home | *funeraria* |
| hospice | *hospicio* |
| hospital | *hospital* |
| mausoleum | *mausoleo* |
| pyre | *pire* |

| | |
|---|---|
| sepulchre | *sepulcro* |
| sepulture | *sepultura* |
| tomb | *tumba* |
| | |
| elegy | *elegía* |
| epitaph | *epitafio* |
| memorial | *memorial* |
| obituary | *obituario* |
| oration (funeral) | *oración* |
| requiem | *réquiem* |
| sarcophagus | *sarcófago* |
| | |
| consoler | *consolador(a)* |
| embalmer | *embalsamador(a)* |
| mortal | *mortal* |
| organ donor | *donante de órgano* |
| survivor | *sobreviviente* |
| widow | *viuda* |
| widower | *viudo* |

# LIFE AFTER DEATH

| | |
|---|---|
| angel | *ángel* |
| heaven | *cielo* |
| heavenly | *celestial* |
| hell | *infierno* |
| life after death | *vida despues de la muerte* |
| paradise | *paraíso* |
| purgatory | *purgatorio* |
| saint | *santo, piadoso* |
| soul | *alma* |
| spirit | *espíritu* |
| spiritual | *espiritual* |

# Satan and Associated Words

| | |
|---|---|
| anti-Christ | *Anti-Cristo* |
| attacks | *atacar* |
| bondage | *esclavitud* |
| counterfeit | *falsificación, falseamiento, remedo* |
| coward | *cobarde* |
| cunning | *astuto* |
| deception | *decepción* |
| demons | *demonios* |
| devil | *diablo* |
| dishonor | *deshonor, desgracia* |
| dragon | *dragón* |
| fairies | *hadas* |
| fall | *caer, caída* |
| fallen angel | *ángel caído* |
| flesh | *carne* |
| king over the realm of the demons | |
| liar | *mentiroso, -a* |
| Lucifer | *Lucifer* |
| murderer | *asesino (a)* |
| old nature | *carácter viejo* |
| originator of evil | *creador de mal, originador de mal* |
| perverse spirits | *espíritus perversos* |
| prince of the powers of the air | *Príncipe de los poderes del aire* |

| | |
|---|---|
| schemes | *esquema, plan* |
| serpent | *serpiente* |
| sin | *pecado* |
| sorcery | *hechicería* |
| strongholds | *fortaleza, baluarte, fortificación, plaza fuerte, punto de apoyo* |
| strongman | *hombre fuerte, forzudo, dictador, hombre de pelo en pecho* |
| subtle | *ingenioso* |
| tarot readings | *naipe tarot* |
| tempter | *tentador* |
| the enemy | *el enemigo* |
| the evil one | *el malvado* |
| the god of this world | *el dios de este mundo* |
| the great deceiver | *el gran engañador* |
| the prince of lies | *príncipe de mentiras* |
| unclean | *sucio, impuro* |
| wicked | *malvado, cruel* |
| witchcraft | *brujería* |
| witches | *brujas* |

# Words for Discussing the Gospel

| English Equivalent | Spanish Word | English Equivalent | Related to |
|---|---|---|---|
| alarm | *la alarma* | to alarm | *alarmar* |
| arm (weapon) | *el arma* | to arm | *armar* |
| help, aid | *la ayuda* | to aid, help, assist | *ayudar* |
| battle | *la batalla* | to battle | *batallar* |
| search, hunt | *la busca* | to seek, search, look for | *buscar* |
| charge, responsibility, burden | *la carga* | to charge, to make responsible, to burden | *cargar* |
| purchase, buy, buying | *la compra* | to buy, purchase | *comparar* |
| copy, duplicate | *la copia* | to copy, duplicate | *copiar* |
| crown | *la corona* | to crown | *coronar* |
| harvest | *la cosecha* | to harvest | *cosechar* |
| criticism | *la critica* | to criticize | *criticar* |
| bill, account, tab | *la cuenta* | to count, charge | *contar* |
| fault | *la culpa* | to blame | *culpar* |
| dance | *la danza, la baile* | to dance | *danzar, bailar* |
| denunciation, accusation | *la denuncia* | to denounce, accuse | *denunciar* |
| defeat | *la derrota* | to defeat | *derrotar* |
| unloading, discharge, discharging | *descarga* | to unload, discharge | *descargar* |
| difference | *la diferencia* | differentiate | *diferenciar* |
| discipline, scourge, whip | *la disciplina* | to discipline, scourge, whip | *disciplinar* |
| excuse | *la disculpa* | to excuse, to ask forgiveness | *disculpar(se)* |

# Frequently Read Bible Verses in Spanish and English from the New International Version of the Bible

| Psalm 23 NIV | Salmo 23 NVI |
|---|---|
| [1]The Lord is my shepherd, I lack nothing. | [1]El Señor es mi pastor, nada me falta; |
| [2]He makes me to lie down in green pastures, | [2]en verdes pastos me hace descansar. |
| He leads me beside quiet waters, | Junto a tranquilas aguas me conduce; |
| [3]he refreshes my soul. | [3]Me infunde nuevas fuerzas. |
| He guides me along right paths | Me guía por sendas de justicia |
| for his name's sake. | Por amor a su nombre |
| [4]Even though I walk through the darkest valley, | [4]Aun si voy por valles tenebrosos, |
| I will fear no evil, | No temo peligro alguno |
| For you are with me; | Porque tu estas a mi lado |
| your rod and your staff, they comfort me. | Tu vara de pastor me reconforta. |
| [5]You prepare a table before me | [5]Dispones ante mi un banquete |
| in the presence of my enemies. | En presencia de mis enemigos. |
| You anoint my head with oil; | Has ungido con perfume mi cabeza; |
| my cup overflows. | Has llenado mi copa a rebosar. |
| [6]Surely goodness and love will follow me all the days of my life, and I will dwell in the house of the LORD forever. | [6]La bondad y el amor me seguirán Todos los días de mi vida; Y en la casa del Señor Habitare para siempre. |

| Psalm 23 KJV | Salmo 23 RVR1960 |
|---|---|
| [1]The Lord is my shepherd; I shall not want. | [1]Jehová es mi pastor; nada me faltará. |
| [2]He maketh me to lie down in green pastures, he leadeth be beside the still waters | [2]En lugares de delicados pastos me hará descansar; Junto a aguas de reposo me pastoreará. |
| [3]he restoreth my soul. He leadeth me in the path of righteousness for his name sake. [4]Ye though I walk in the valley of the shadow of death I will fear no evil for though art with me. They rod and they staff they comfort me. | [3]Confortará mi alma; Me guiará por sendas de justicia por amor de su nombre. [4]Aunque ande en valle de sombra de muerte, No temeré mal alguno, porque tú estarás conmigo; Tu vara y tu cayado me infundirán aliento. |
| [5]Thou prepareth a table before me in the presence of mine enemies. Though annointeth thy head with oil my cup runneth over. Surly your goodness and mercy shall follow me all the days of my life. And I shall dwell in the house of the Lord forever. | [5]Aderezas mesa delante de mí en presencia de mis angustiadores; Unges mi cabeza con aceite; mi copa está rebosando. [6]Ciertamente el bien y la misericordia me seguirán todos los días de mi vida, Y en la casa de Jehová moraré por largos días. |

# LORD'S PRAYER

| Matthew 6:9-13 NIV | Mateo 6:9-13 NVI |
|---|---|
| ⁹This, then, is how you should pray; "'Our Father in heaven hallowed be your name ¹⁰Your kingdom come your will be done on Earth as it is in heaven ¹¹Give us today our daily bread. ¹²And forgive us our debts, as we also have forgiven our debtors. ¹³And lead us not into temptation, but deliver us from the evil one, for yours is the kingdom and the power and the glory forever. Amen". | ⁹Ustedes deben orar así: "Padre nuestro que esta en el cielo Santificado sea tu nombre, ¹⁰Venga tu reino hágase tu voluntad en la tierra como en el cielo ¹¹Danos hoy nuestro pan cotidiano ¹²perdónanos nuestras deudas como también nosotros hemos Perdonado a nuestros deudores ¹³Y no nos dejes caer en tentación sino líbranos de maligno, porque tuyos son el reino y el poder y la gloria para siempre. Amén". |
| **Matthew 6-13 KJV** | **Mateo 6-13 RVR1960** |
| 9After this manner therefore pray ye: Our Father which art in heaven, Hallowed be thy name. 10 Thy kingdom come, Thy will be done in earth, as it is in heaven. 11 Give us this day our daily bread. 12 And forgive us our debts, as we forgive our debtors. 13 And lead us not into temptation, but deliver us from evil: For thine is the kingdom, and the power, and the glory, for ever. Amen. | 9 Vosotros, pues, oraréis así: Padre nuestro que estás en los cielos, santificado sea tu nombre. 10 Venga tu reino. Hágase tu voluntad, como en el cielo, así también en la tierra. 11 El pan nuestro de cada día, dánoslo hoy. 12 Y perdónanos nuestras deudas, como también nosotros perdonamos a nuestros deudores. 13 Y no nos metas en tentación, mas líbranos del mal; porque tuyo es el reino, y el poder, y la gloria, por todos los siglos. Amén. |

# REFERENCES

Thomas, S., Nash, R., Thomas, G., and Richmond, D. (2005). *The Big Red Book of Spanish Vocabulary*, McGraw Hill.

\* List of words from *Prayers that Rout Demons: Prayers for Defeating Demons and Overthrowing the Power of Darkness* by John Eckhardt (2008). Lake Mary, FL: Charisma Press.

# EXTRA WORDS AND NOTES

# EXTRA WORDS AND NOTES

_____

_____

_____

_____

_____

_____

_____

_____

_____

_____

_____

_____

_____

# EXTRA WORDS AND NOTES

# EXTRA WORDS AND NOTES

# EXTRA WORDS AND NOTES

_____

_____

_____

_____

_____

_____

_____

_____

_____

_____

_____

_____

_____

_____

Printed in the United States
by Baker & Taylor Publisher Services